WHAT'S THE BIG IDEA?

Also by Vicki Cobb:

Bangs and Twangs: Science Fun with Sound

Feeling Your Way: Discover Your Sense of Touch

Follow Your Nose: Discover Your Sense of Smell

Harry Houdini: A Photographic Story of a Life

How to Really Fool Yourself

Light Action! Amazing Experiments with Optics

Marie Curie: A Photographic Story of a Life

Open Your Eyes: Discover Your Sense of Sight

Perk Up Your Ears: Discover Your Sense of Hearing

Science Experiments You Can Eat

Sources of Forces: Science Fun with Force Fields

Squirts and Spurts: Science Fun with Water

We Dare You! Hundreds of Fun Science Bets, Challenges, and Experiments You Can Do at Home

Where's the Science Here? Fireworks

Where's the Science Here? Junk Food

Where's the Science Here? On Stage

Where's the Science Here? Sneakers

Whirlers and Twirlers: Science Fun with Spinning

Your Body Battles a Broken Bone

Your Body Battles a Cavity

Your Body Battles a Cold

Your Body Battles an Earache

Your Body Battles a Skinned Knee

Your Body Battles a Stomachache

Your Tongue Can Tell: Discover Your Sense of Taste

WHAT'S THE BIG IDEA?

Amazing Science Questions for the Curious Kid

VICKI COBB

Skyhorse Publishing

Skyhorse Publishing books may be purchased in bulk at special discounts for sales promotion, corporate gifts, fund-raising, or educational purposes. Special editions can also be created to specifications. For details, contact the Special Sales Department, Skyhorse Publishing, 555 Eighth Avenue, Suite 903, New York, NY 10018 or info@skyhorsepublishing.com.

www.skyhorsepublishing.com

10 9 8 7 6 5 4 3 2 1

Library of Congress Cataloging-in-Publication Data

Cobb, Vicki.
  What's the big idea? : amazing science questions for curious kids / Vicki Cobb.
      p. cm.
  ISBN 978-1-61608-013-6 (hardcover : alk. paper)
  1. Science--Miscellanea--Juvenile literature. I. Title.
  Q163.C688 2010
  500--dc22
                                    2009046866

Printed in China

CONTENTS

WHAT'S A BIG IDEA?

A big idea is one that has no simple or easy answer. There are four big ideas in this book: motion, energy, matter, and life. The motion of nonliving objects—rolling balls, falling stones, the moon, and stars—seems so ordinary and familiar that most people take it for granted. Matter, on the other hand, comes in so many different forms—solids, liquids, gases, metals, nonmetals, living material—that it is hard to imagine what any of these forms have in common. Energy is an idea that is in the news just about every day, yet most people couldn't tell you what the big idea of energy is. And life—what life is—seems mind-boggling and infinitely complicated. How do you bend your brain around it?

Science tackles big ideas. How? The same way you eat an elephant: one bite at a time. Science goes after big ideas by asking simpler questions that *can* be answered by *doing something*. If you ask a scientist, "How do you know?" a scientist doesn't say, "I just know," or "Everyone knows," or "I read it someplace." A scientist says, "This is what I did. If you do what I did, you'll know what I know." In other words, scientists answer their questions by doing experiments that anyone can check. And each question is like one tiny bite of the elephant. Every answer leads to more questions to be answered by more experiments, and on and on. Scientific knowledge builds bit by bit with contributions by many people. Every once in a while there is a big breakthrough and we get the big idea. All of this takes time.

Science itself is a big idea. Before there was science people believed what they saw, heard, tasted, felt, and smelled. They believed their senses and they believed their experiences. Yet it turned out that some of their big ideas were just plain wrong. They believed, for example, that the Earth was the center of the universe, that the moon and stars were perfect and the Earth was imperfect, and that everything was made of four elements: earth, air, fire, and water. Modern science began about four hundred years ago when an

Italian mathematician, Galileo Galilei, began by asking some seemingly dumb questions about motion, such as, "Why does a rolling ball stop rolling?" He came up with some surprising answers that challenged what most people assumed to be true. You'll get a chance to discover his thinking in this book. It will blow your mind!

Scientists learn by asking questions. Often they have to figure out a clever way to get an answer. Sometimes they have to live a long time without knowing the answer. Most kids ask questions in order to get answers fast. (Do you stop asking questions when you get an answer?) This book is designed to make you stop and think about each question before reading the answer. That's why there is a whole page just for the question. Then you'll find out what scientists have learned that answers the question. You'll be able to do simple things to see the answer for yourself (and not just take my word for it). You can build your own scientific knowledge by reading one question at a time and thinking about it before rushing on to the next question. By the time you've finished this book, you'll have a pretty good idea of what science is about. It will help you understand what you learn in school.

If you're a curious kid, you may want to think about becoming a scientist. One very famous scientist is Isidor Isaac Rabi (1898–1988). Rabi discovered the big idea that makes it possible to look inside the human body in MRI scans in a hospital, which helps diagnose many diseases and injuries. He won the Nobel Prize in Physics in 1944. He owes his success in science to his mother. Every day, when he came home from school, she would ask him, "What good question did you ask today?" I hope that this book gets you started asking some good questions, yourself.

Before there was science, people could only imagine doing impossible things. Magicians waved a wand and "Presto!" something happened that defied what everyone knew to be real. Today, you wave a wand to turn on a screen that shows a moving picture of an event on the other side of the world. You take the TV remote for granted. Soon you'll be able to operate the TV just by waving your hand at the screen. People who lived only a hundred years ago would have been amazed! Technology, the use of scientific knowledge, proves the power of science. And it all starts by asking questions, one bite at a time, which turns out to be not so dumb after all.

WHAT'S THE BIG IDEA?

BIG IDEA: MOTION IS NOT WHAT IT APPEARS TO BE

WHY DOES A ROLLING BALL STOP ROLLING?

Four hundred years ago, an Italian mathematician, Galileo (Ga-li-LAY-oh) (1564–1642), did a thought experiment about this. He concluded that rolling balls should never stop rolling. That they do didn't make sense to him. Do Galileo's thought experiment yourself (use your imagination) to see why.

Check it out:

Imagine how a ball rolls up a hill after you give it a little push. It rolls slower and slower until it stops for a moment, then rolls back downhill. Now, imagine how the ball rolls downhill. It goes faster and faster. Think about this: If the ball rolling uphill slows down, and the ball rolling downhill speeds up, how should it roll if there is no hill? A ball rolling on level ground should not speed up or slow down. It should go at the same speed forever!

But that's not what happens in real life. Balls rolling on level ground do come to a stop sooner or later. Something must be stopping them. What is it?

A hundred years after Galileo, an Englishman named Isaac Newton (1643–1727) did some more thinking about this. It's obvious that a resting ball will rest forever. It will remain resting until it is hit by some outside force that will make it move. That's easy to understand. But Newton figured out that this same rule is true for balls that are already in motion. Once a ball is moving, it will keep on moving forever unless it is stopped by some force. In other words, just as a push or pull is needed to make resting objects *start* moving, a push or pull is needed to make moving objects *stop* moving.

Any ball that stops rolling must have a force stopping it. What is it? It's not a force that's easy to see. As it turns out, the force that slows the ball acts at the point where the ball touches the surface it's rolling on. This force is called *friction.* Friction is a force that occurs between two surfaces where there is motion. It works against that motion. If you could design a machine without friction, it would move forever. Many have tried to make such a perpetual-motion machine. All have failed.

Newton and Galileo's answer to this seemingly dumb question explains why all balls and other nonliving objects either move or don't move. It is called Newton's First Law of Motion:

Moving objects will move forever and resting objects will rest forever, unless some outside force acts on them.

HOW DO WE KNOW THE EARTH IS MOVING WHEN IT LOOKS LIKE THE SKY IS MOVING?

How do you know when you are moving? You feel bumps and shakes. You feel the wind in your face and see the scenery passing by.

This was the problem that faced early astronomers. They saw the sun move across the sky by day, and the stars move across by night. They saw the moon rise and set. It was easier to think that the Earth was not moving and that everything else in the heavens moved around it. After all, that's the way it looks.

Almost 2,000 years ago, a Greek astronomer named Ptolemy (TAHL-a-me) (c. 90–168 AD) said that the Earth was the center of the universe and the moon, sun, stars, and planets all moved around it. Travelers needed to know where the heavenly bodies would be, since they used them to find their way. Ptolemy predicted correctly enough where they could be found. His system was used for 1,400 years.

About 450 years ago, a Polish astronomer named Copernicus (Co-PER-ni-cuss) (1473–1543) had a different idea. Ptolemy made some mistakes

predicting where planets would be. Copernicus figured that the universe would be a lot simpler if all the planets, including the Earth, moved around the sun.

At first, this idea of Copernicus's was not popular. It went against what people saw with their own eyes. Telescopes had not yet been invented. Copernicus had no proof that the Earth moved. But he knew what the proof would be.

Check out this thought experiment:

Suppose that your ride is perfectly smooth and there is no wind. Imagine that you are in a boat in the middle of a perfectly calm sea. In the distance, you see another boat passing you. How would you know if you are moving more slowly than the other boat, or if you are still and the other boat is moving past you? The answer is that you would have no way of knowing. You could be moving or you could not be moving.

We look at the stars each night as the Earth moves around the sun. The stars are grouped into well-known patterns called *constellations.* Constellations, like the Big Dipper, seem to always be the same. Copernicus believed that some of the stars in a constellation were nearer to the Earth than others. He believed that the pattern of the stars in a constellation changed a tiny bit as the Earth moved around the sun. This change, he thought, proved that the Earth moved.

Here's the reasoning behind Copernicus's thinking: If the stars in a constellation are different distances from Earth, you could think of the far stars as background to the closer stars. . . . Say you look at Big Dipper on March 6th. Then you look at it on September 6th. In six months the Earth has moved halfway around the sun. It is as far away as it can get from its position six months earlier. Just as the background shifts behind your fingers as you shift your eyes, so too the pattern of the background stars compared to the foreground stars shifts between these two views. Copernicus knew that the changes in the distances between the stars would be tiny. They would be hard to see because the stars were so far away. But after the telescope was invented, astronomers measured the changing patterns of the stars as the Earth moved. We now have our proof. The name of the proof is "stellar parallax." The word "stellar" means "stars." So if someone asks you how

Check it out:

Point your index finger upward about a foot from the end of your nose. Look at your finger as you open and close each eye in turn. You will see your finger appear to jump back and forth compared to the background. This is because each eye sees the background behind your finger from a different position. This phenomenon is called "ocular parallax." Ocular means "eyes" we know that the earth moves around the sun, your answer is the "stellar parallax." Be ready to explain. They'll think you're sooooo smart!

But the motion of the Earth around the sun does not explain how the sun and the moon rise and set. So Copernicus said that the Earth has two kinds of motion. The Earth also spins like a top while it is traveling around the sun. The spinning of the Earth makes the sun appear to move across the sky by day, and it makes the starry sky and moon seem to rise and set at night.

IF THE EARTH IS SPINNING, WHY DON'T WE FEEL IT MOVE?

We don't feel the Earth move because it is spinning at a steady rate, so the ride is perfectly smooth. We feel motion only when there is a *change* in the way we are moving. And a change in motion occurs only when an outside force acts on us. (Remember Newton's First Law.)

Everything on the Earth's surface is moving with the Earth.

When you are sitting in a moving car, you have the same forward movement as the car. If the car suddenly crashes to a stop, you keep this forward motion and can be thrown through the windshield. That's why we wear seat belts!

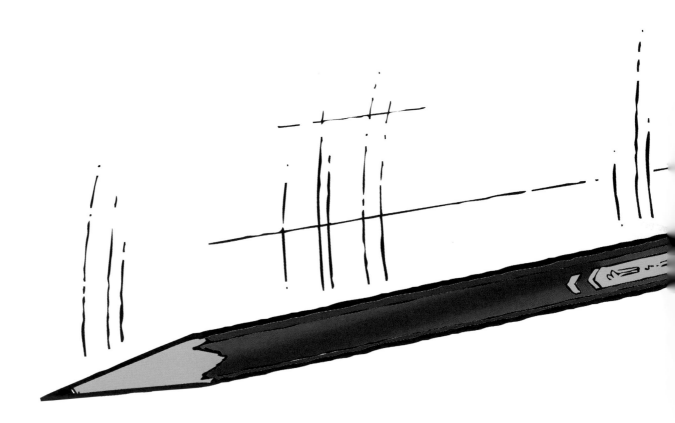

Check it out:

The next time you ride in a car, ask the driver to go at a steady speed. Drop a pencil on the floor while you are moving. Later, when the car is not moving, drop the pencil exactly the same way. Both times it will land on the same spot. The motion of the car does not change the fall of the pencil, as long as that motion is steady. Only a sudden change in the car's motion, while you are dropping the pencil, will change the landing spot.

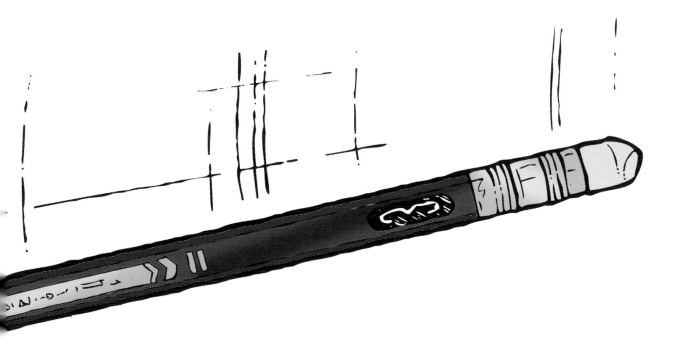

WHICH FALLS FASTER, A BOWLING BALL OR A MARBLE?

The idea that heavier objects fall faster than lighter ones is another one of those great mistakes that people believed for centuries. An ancient Greek named Aristotle (AR-is-tot-ul) (384–322 BC) was the first to write this theory down. Aristotle said that if one stone weighed ten pounds and another stone weighed one pound, the ten-pound stone would fall ten times faster.

Aristotle was a very important thinker and writer. Many people believed Aristotle was right about everything. No one tested his ideas.

It's easy to test the idea that heavy objects fall faster than light ones.

Galileo lived 2,000 years after Aristotle and he took a whole new look at the questions. There is a story that Galileo dropped two different weights off the Leaning Tower of Pisa, which may or may not be true. But we do know that Galileo was very clever in the way he measured how things fall.

GALILEO

Check this out with a friend:

One of you should drop two objects of different weights, like a baseball and a marble, at the same time. You might drop them off a porch or a jungle gym. Have your friend stand on the ground at a safe distance to see which one reaches the ground first. Listen for the sound when they hit the ground. You should get a tie every time. If you don't, then you didn't drop the two items at the same time. The only time there is an exception is when you drop something like a feather that catches the air.

When Galileo lived, about 400 years ago, there were no watches or clocks. Any falling object fell too fast for him to measure how long it took. So Galileo decided to slow down falling objects. Instead of dropping objects off buildings, he decided to roll balls down a ramp. He figured that the same force that made things fall would make balls roll down a ramp. This force is called *gravity.* A ramp would make it easier to see gravity in action. He measured the time by

catching drops of water while a ball rolled. He could change the steepness of the ramp and measure the distance the ball traveled while water dripped. The steepest ramp was very close to a freefall.

Galileo did lots of experiments. He made an incredible discovery.

3 SECONDS

No matter how heavy or light they are, all balls fall toward the Earth at the same rate!

Galileo also discovered how to ask questions that could be answered by experiments in his laboratory. This is the way scientists collect information. For this reason, Galileo is called the father of modern science.

WHY CAN'T YOU STAND AN EGG ON ITS END?

You can't stand an egg on its end because of the way gravity makes things fall. Gravity is a force of attraction between the Earth and objects on or near its surface. When gravity pulls on a ball, it is as if the center of the Earth is attracting the center of the ball. An egg doesn't have a regular shape like a ball. So gravity pulls on the point of the egg that *seems* to be its center. This spot is called the egg's *center of gravity*.

An egg's center of gravity is not at the center of the egg. An object falls toward the center of the Earth. It would keep going if there were a hole to fall into. It is as if the object were trying to get its center of gravity as close as possible to the Earth's center of gravity. An egg will rest on its side because its curved surface makes it easy to move. And when it rolls on its side its center of gravity is as low as it can get and as close as it can get to the Earth's center of gravity.

KEEPING YOUR CENTER OF GRAVITY LINED UP OVER YOUR FEET IS A BALANCING ACT.

WHY DOESN'T THE MOON FALL TO EARTH?

Gravity is the force pulling the moon and the Earth together, just as gravity is the force pulling an egg and the Earth together. If gravity were the only force acting on the moon, it would crash into the Earth. The moon doesn't fall into the Earth because there's an equal force sending the moon off into space.

This force comes from the motion of the moon. If gravity suddenly disappeared, the moon would fly off in a straight line.

The combination of the force pulling an object toward the center and the motion of the whirling object seems to create another force. It is called *centrifugal force*, meaning "away from the center." Actually, centrifugal force is the absence of a force toward the center.

Gravity and the straight-line motion of the moon work together to trap the moon in a circular path around the Earth. This path is called an *orbit*.

Isaac Newton figured out why the moon doesn't fall to the Earth. There is a story about this discovery. Newton was lying under an apple tree, thinking about the moon. He

PATH WHEN RELEASED

Check out this thought experiment:

Imagine whirling a ball at the end of a string. The string is a force holding the ball in its path around the center, just like gravity acts on the moon. When you let go, the ball flies off in a straight line. If you wanted to make the whirling ball fly to a target, you would have to time your release very accurately.

You can feel centrifugal force sending blood into your fingertips when you swing your arms in a circle. Your arms won't fly off because they're attached to your body. Your blood is loose, so it starts to move off into space until it is stopped by your fingertips. Since your blood is warm, whirling your arms is a good way to warm your hands in winter.

was wondering why it wasn't falling. An apple fell from the tree. Newton looked at the falling apple and suddenly realized the moon *is* falling. But the fall is constantly being stopped by the moon's straight-line motion into space.

The moon keeps moving because there is no friction to slow it down. If there were no forces acting on the moon, its motion would carry it out of our solar system. Gravity constantly keeps the direction of the moon's motion in a circular orbit.

Newton added this idea—how forces can change the direction of motion—to his First Law of Motion:

Moving objects will keep moving forever *in a straight line*, and resting objects will rest forever, unless some outside force acts on them.

The same forces keep man-made satellites in orbit. Space engineers figure that a satellite has to go about five miles each second to stay in an orbit about a hundred miles from the Earth's surface. A speed of seven miles each second is fast enough to escape the pull of the Earth's gravity and send a spacecraft into space.

WE SAY THAT
AN APPLE FALLS
DOWN TO EARTH.
WHY DOESN'T THE
EARTH FALL UP TO
THE APPLE?

Believe it or not, the Earth *is* falling up to an apple, moved by the same force that causes the apple to fall down to Earth. Since the Earth is so huge by comparison, you can't see the Earth's attraction to the apple.

Isaac Newton was the first person to think about this seemingly dumb question. When Newton saw an apple fall and thought about the moon falling to Earth, he began to really think about gravity. Newton said that gravity was a force of attraction between objects. Every bit of matter has gravity and is attracted to every other bit of matter. The pull of gravity can go across space. So the apple pulls the Earth up as the Earth pulls the apple down. But gravity is a very weak force. It isn't felt unless you have a huge

amount of matter gathered together in a body as big as the Earth or the moon. Newton's idea about gravity is that gravity pulls the Earth and the moon together, just as it pulls the Earth and the apple together.

The apple is so small and has so little gravity that it's impossible to detect its pull on the Earth. But the pull of the moon's gravity causes the tides of the ocean. The water on Earth *is falling up* toward the moon!

Newton summed up his ideas about gravity being a two-way street in his Third Law of Motion:

Every action has an equal and opposite reaction.

WHICH TAKES LONGER, A BIG, HIGH SWING OR A SMALL, LOW SWING?

Your experiments will help you discover that a big swing takes exactly the same amount of time as a small swing!

Galileo discovered this rule for a swinging object. One day he was in church. A lamplighter had just lit a lamp that was hanging from the ceiling. It was swinging back and forth. Galileo wondered if a big swing

Check it out:

Go with a friend to a playground that has swings. Have your friend start counting at a steady rate the moment you give an empty swing a good hard push. Your friend should count with his or her back to the swing. At the end of the fifth swing, tell your friend to stop counting.

Now repeat your experiment. But this time give the swing a tiny push, just enough to set it swinging back and forth. Again, tell your friend to stop counting after five swings. Did your friend count to almost the same number each time? Keep on experimenting. What happens when you count ten high swings and ten low ones? What happens when you use a watch with a second hand instead of a friend who counts? What happens when someone is sitting on the swing?

would take longer than a little swing. Since he didn't have a watch or a friend to count for him, he used his own heartbeat. Galileo felt his pulse as he counted lamp swings. He discovered that the lamp always took the same amount of time to swing back and forth, even though the swings got smaller and smaller.

WHAT IS A SWINGING OBJECT GOOD FOR?

A freely swinging object is called a *pendulum*. A pendulum swings with a regular beat. Why not use it to measure time? Remember, in the days of Galileo there were no clocks or watches as we know them. Galileo had to measure short amounts of time by catching drips of water. A pendulum became another way to count short bits of time.

At first, pendulums were used only to time people's pulses. Later, inventors used pendulums to make all kinds of clocks.

A pendulum can also prove that the Earth turns. In 1851, French scientist Jean Foucault (foo-KO) (1819–1868) hung an iron-ball pendulum from the top of a dome in a large building. Marks on the floor made it seem as if the swinging pendulum slowly changed direction. Actually it was swinging back and forth in a straight line. The Earth was turning underneath the pendulum.

WHAT DOES IT TAKE TO MOVE A PIANO?

A piano is a heavy object that resists being moved. The resistance of an object to being moved is called *inertia*. A piano won't move unless it is pushed hard enough to overcome its inertia. The push also has to be strong enough to overcome the friction between the piano and the floor. If you want to lift the piano, then the force you use has to overcome its weight. Weight is the force of gravity on an object.

Whenever a force moves something like a piano, scientists say that *work* has been done. If you try to move a piano, no matter how much you huff and puff, you haven't done any work if it doesn't move. Scientists are very particular about the idea of work. Work is accomplished only when matter is moved.

Now the question is: What does it take to do work? The answer sounds simple, but there are many ways of thinking about this. For scientists, the key part of any answer is that it takes *energy* to do work. Energy can come from many sources. It can come from muscles, or an engine, or a wall socket. Whenever you see an object changing its speed or moving against a force, it's because of energy. The energy of motion is called *kinetic energy,* and all moving objects have it.

HOW IS A WOUND-UP SPRING LIKE THE TOP OF A WATERFALL?

Both a wound-up spring in a watch or a toy and the water at the top of a waterfall have stored energy. Stored energy isn't doing any work. When the water falls, the energy is released as kinetic energy. If the water falls on a water wheel, it makes the wheel turn. The kinetic energy of a turning water wheel can then move a millstone or turn a turbine to generate electricity. The kinetic energy is now doing useful work. When a spring unwinds, it can also do useful work. It can move the hands of a watch or make a toy car run. Machines are inventions that use energy for useful work.

Sometimes work is done to store energy. When you climb the ladder of a slide you do work—lifting up your body. When you are sitting at the top of the slide your body has stored energy, just like the water at the top of a waterfall. This energy is released as kinetic energy when you move down the slide. But the kinetic energy of your sliding body is not being used to do useful work because it is not doing some other job.

DO HOT THINGS WEIGH MORE THAN COLD THINGS?

People used to think that heat was a kind of fluid. They believed that when things cooled off the heat fluid escaped into the air. As a result, they believed that hot things should weigh more than cold things. But when they did experiments weighing hot things and cold things to see if hot things weighed more, the scales didn't show any difference. They made better and better scales, but they still didn't see any difference. An object weighed exactly the same no matter how hot or cold it was. People needed a new way to think about heat.

Count Benjamin Thompson Rumford (1753–1814) was one of the people who tried to measure the weight of heat. He was an American who sympathized with the British and moved to England after the American Revolution. He had the job of supervising the making of cannons. He noticed that the metal of a brass cannon got very hot when it was being hollowed out. Could it be that the motion of the tool used to hollow out the cannon caused the heat? Rumford was the first person to think that motion and heat might be the same thing.

Are motion and heat the same thing?

If motion can produce heat, is the opposite true? Can heat produce motion and do work? You bet! The steam engine is one kind of machine that changes the heat energy released by burning wood into steam that runs a locomotive.

Fuels also have stored energy, which is sometimes called *chemical energy.* Chemical energy is released as heat and light when the fuel burns during a chemical reaction.

Check it out:

Rub your hands together quickly and see how they get warmer.

So the question of whether hot things weigh more than cold things was not so dumb after all. It led to the important idea that one kind of energy can change into another kind. Energy can take many forms. In addition to heat, kinetic, and chemical energy, other kinds of energy are sound, light, and electricity.

Some of the devices that change one kind of energy into another are a toaster, which changes electricity into heat; a TV, which turns electricity into light and sound; a wind-up alarm clock, which transforms kinetic energy into sound; and a car, which turns chemical energy (burning fuel) into heat and, in turn, into kinetic energy.

Electricity is one of the easiest kinds of energy for us to use. But usable electricity doesn't exist in nature. That's the big problem with electricity. Electricity has to be manufactured from other kinds of energy. Falling water or burning coal or oil is used to make electricity at power plants. And each kind of energy used to produce electricity has a downside (more on this later).

DOES WATER THAT BOILS FASTER COOK FASTER?

As the pot sits over the flame on the burner, the water begins moving. The temperature goes up, and the water moves faster and faster. Tiny bubbles start forming on the bottom of the pot. These are not air bubbles but water that has changed into a gas called *steam*.

The tiny steam bubbles rise to the surface as the water starts to boil. The thermometer reads 212 degrees on the Fahrenheit thermometer and 100 degrees on the Celsius thermometer. The bubbles get larger and the water moves more and more rapidly. Finally, it reaches a rolling boil. The temperature stays at exactly 212 degrees Fahrenheit, or 100 degrees Celsius, and never changes!

Since slowly boiling water is at the same temperature as water at a rolling boil, you can guess the answer to the question. Fast boiling water cooks at exactly the same rate as slowly boiling, or simmering, water.

The heat energy from the burner starts making the water move. This motion is a clue to what heat is all about. Scientists think that heat is the motion of the smallest particles of matter—molecules. As water molecules are heated, they start moving faster and faster. You see the temperature rise.

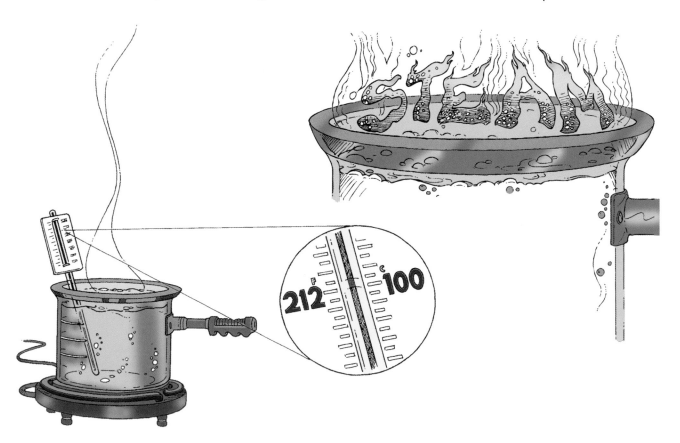

Check it out:

If you have a cook's thermometer, you can watch what happens when you heat water in a pot. (Don't try to boil water without having an adult present.)

When the temperature reaches 212°F, or 100°C, the water molecules are moving fast enough to escape from the water's surface as steam. Now the heat energy changes the water into steam. But the temperature of the water won't change until it has all been changed to steam.

HOW DOES A POT HOLDER WORK?

More energy is needed to overcome the inertia of some objects than others. The same thing is true of molecules. It takes more energy to move certain kinds of molecules than other kinds. The speed of molecules is measured as temperature. Some materials get hot more easily than others because their molecules are moved more easily. Metals get hot very easily. For this reason they are called *heat conductors*. A metal pot handle can get too hot to touch. If you put a metal spoon in a cup of hot coffee, its handle will soon begin to feel warm. Try this and see.☺

Check it out:

Get a paper cup, a Styrofoam cup, and a foil baking cup. Put an ice cube in each. See which ice cube melts fastest. The best insulator protects the cube from the heat in the air, and that cube will melt the slowest.

Other materials absorb heat without getting hot. These materials are called *insulators*. Most nonmetals and air are good insulators. Fabric is a good insulator. When you wrap a hot pot handle in a pot holder, the pot holder acts as an insulator. Your hand is protected. So a potholder doesn't do work according to the definition of work I gave you earlier. I was using the word "work" here in an unscientific way. Styrofoam is another good heat insulator.

A THERMOS BOTTLE KEEPS THINGS WARM OR COLD BY INSULATING WITH A VACUUM.

WHY IS THE SKY BLUE? WHY NOT GREEN OR YELLOW?

First of all, the sky is black at night, when there is no sunlight. So the color of the sky depends on light, which is a kind of energy. Light from the sun appears to be white. But you can see a clue to its real nature when a rainbow forms. A rainbow is sunlight broken up into many different colors: red, orange, yellow, green, blue, and violet. All these different colors make up the visible light *spectrum*. When we see the whole spectrum combined, we are seeing white light.

Matter reflects light. (If it didn't you couldn't see it. Everything you see is reflected light.) A mirror reflects almost all the light that strikes it, while a red object reflects only red light. Air particles reflect light in all directions, scattering it. The colors that are scattered the most are violet and blue. Our eyes are not as sensitive to violet, so we see the sky as blue.

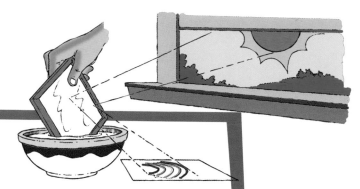

Check it out:

All you need is a cereal dish filled with water about two inches deep, a small hand mirror, a sheet of white paper, and a sunny day to break up sunlight into the spectrum.

   Put the dish of water in the sunlight. Put one end of the mirror in the water. You can easily make a bright spot of light reflect off the mirror onto the piece of paper. Then change the tilt of the mirror until you capture a spectrum on your piece of paper. The red and yellow will be at the top ends and the green, blue, and violet at the bottom.

WHO EVER HEARD OF LIGHT YOU CAN'T SEE?

The only way we can know about energy is by what it does to matter. For example, energy moves matter, raises its temperature, changes it from a solid to a liquid or from a liquid to a gas, and changes its color. We see light because we have nerves in our eyes that react to it. But our eyes are not able to detect the entire spectrum. The light our eyes cannot see must be detected in some other way. The trick is to find a substance on which light can be recorded, like film in a camera or an electronic image sensor in a digital camera.

Film in a camera is coated with a substance that turns dark when light strikes it. Patterns of light and shadow from the real world show up as pictures on film. Can film detect light that our eyes are not able to see? Absolutely! One person who detected invisible light rays was a French scientist named Antoine Henri Becquerel (beck-KRel) (1852–1908). In 1896, Becquerel

wrapped photographic film in light-proof black paper. He put a mineral containing uranium on top of the wrapped film. When he developed the film, he found a cloudy area under the mineral. The mineral was giving off invisible rays that could pass through the paper. These invisible rays are called *radioactivity*. Photographic film shows that there is light we cannot see at both the red and the violet ends of the spectrum.

Check it out:

Put a sheet of black paper and a sheet of white paper in bright sunlight. After five minutes, feel both pieces of paper. Which one feels warmer?

The invisible light next to the violet end is called *ultraviolet*. Ultraviolet light from the sun will cause your skin to become sunburned. Next to the red end of the spectrum is the invisible *infrared* light. Black objects absorb more infrared light than do white objects:

X-rays are invisible rays next to ultraviolet in the spectrum. They can pass through the soft parts of your body and take pictures of your bones.

Microwaves are next to infrared rays. In a microwave oven, energy from the microwave makes water molecules move faster, so food gets hot and cooks quickly.

WHAT DOES ENERGY WEIGH?

For many years scientists believed that only matter had weight. They thought that energy was completely different from matter and weighed nothing. Then, at the beginning of the twentieth century, Albert Einstein (1879–1955) came along and changed the way everyone thought about matter and energy.

Einstein said that matter and energy were the same thing! Energy equals matter that has been multiplied by a huge number, bigger than you can imagine. Enormous amounts of energy can be released from a tiny bit of matter. So, according to Einstein, energy weighs so little that it can't be measured; only calculated. The important thought is that energy, which equals matter, weighs something. Only certain kinds of matter change into energy in nature.

One type of matter that changes into energy is a radioactive material such as uranium. Little pieces of uranium atoms break off and release energy in the process. The invisible rays photographed by Antoine-Henri Becquerel are this type of energy. Some of the rays are like X-rays and can pass through skin into the body where they can cause harm. Uranium atoms fall apart all by themselves. But to make an atom bomb, scientists deliberately split atoms. Uranium atoms are split into bigger pieces than what would chip off naturally, so even more matter changes into huge amounts of energy.

Nuclear energy, the energy that comes from splitting uranium atoms, is both heat energy and invisible light in the form of dangerous radiation. Nuclear power plants use the heat to make steam

that generates electricity. Radioactivity from uranium—the fuel for nuclear power plants—is dangerous. Extra care must be taken so that deadly radiation doesn't escape into the air.

Some people are against nuclear energy because of its dangers. Everyone wants electricity, but almost every kind of energy used to make electricity has problems.

Where dams are built to make waterfalls, the falling water generates electricity at hydroelectric plants. But the lakes formed by the dams cover valuable land. So some people are against these dams. Other power plants burn oil and gas. There is a limited amount of these clean-burning fuels but they all add carbon dioxide to the air. This extra carbon dioxide is a cause of global warming. Some plants burn coal. Untreated smoke from these plants can cause acid rain, which pollutes the land. People protest the fuel-burning plants. They worry about what happens when oil and gas are used up. Scientists are designing ways to use the wind, the tides, the sun, and the heat from the ocean as sources of clean energy that won't contribute to global warming. Their inventions will be the source of energy for the future. Practical answers are on the horizon. The world is going green.

WHY DOESN'T THE SUN BURN OUT?

The secret of the sun's constant energy is that it is not fire. A fire is a chemical reaction that lasts until all the fuel is used up. The sun's energy is a kind of nuclear energy but it is not the splitting of heavy atoms. It is the fusing of hydrogen atoms, the lightest gas in the universe, on the sun to make atoms of helium, the second lightest gas in the universe. A helium atom weighs slightly less than the two atoms of hydrogen that made it. This difference in mass is released as energy—tremendous amounts of energy.

The hydrogen bomb, which is far more powerful than the atom bomb, depends on *nuclear fusion.* Nuclear fusion takes place at extremely hot temperatures, such as those created by an atom bomb. In fact, the trigger for the hydrogen bomb is an atom bomb. The amount of heat energy released by fusion is so great that all matter that comes near it is vaporized. Scientists have not yet found a way to use fusion for peaceful purposes.

Our sun is about four and a half billion years old. Scientists figure that it will continue to give off energy steadily for another five billion years or so, before it goes into its old age.

BIG IDEA: MATTER IS MADE OF SIMPLER STUFF

WHICH WEIGHS MORE, A POUND OF FEATHERS OR A POUND OF GOLD?

Of course a pound of feathers and a pound of gold weigh exactly the same! But if you held a pound of gold in one hand and a pound of feathers in the other, the gold would feel heavier. Your sense of touch can fool you. The feathers take up a lot more space than the gold. You expect something that is larger to weigh more than something that is smaller, so when it doesn't, the smaller object feels heavier.

Gold is much denser than feathers. *Density* is the amount of material, or *matter*, that is packed into a certain space or volume. If you could pack the feathers into the same volume as the gold, they would have exactly the same density. The feathers would feel as heavy as the gold.

Gold is a very dense metal. A gold chain will feel a lot heavier than one that is not made of gold.

Check it out:

Lift gold jewelry. Then lift jewelry that seems to take up the same amount of space but is made of different materials. Can you feel the differences in weight?

Gold is one of the densest kinds of matter on Earth. Its density makes it easy to collect from dirt or sand by panning. Anyone can pan for gold. All you do is mix the sand or dirt containing gold with water in a pan. You swish the pan around. The sand or dirt washes over the side of the pan with the water, and the gold sinks to the bottom. Even tiny flakes, called gold dust, sink to the bottom. If you keep adding water and swishing off the dirt, soon only the gold is left in the pan.

If you're lucky, you might find a flake or two in a pan of dirt. When gold was discovered in California, many people caught "gold fever." They panned day and night to collect gold dust. They found gold, but many of them did not get rich. Their efforts did not "pan" out.

The densest material in the universe is a black hole, which is not really a hole. It is the densest kind of matter. A piece of black hole the size of a pea would weigh more than the entire Earth!

HOW CAN YOU MAKE GOLD?

You can't make gold, plain and simple. But hundreds of years ago, some people believed that you could make gold out of other metals, like iron or copper. So they mixed and stirred and heated all kinds of things. They discovered that the only way to end up with gold was to start with gold. They couldn't make gold from anything else because gold is one of the simplest materials on Earth. It is an *element*.

There are ninety-two elements in nature. Maybe you already know some of them. Here are a few examples: silver, oxygen, nitrogen, hydrogen, carbon, iron, and neon. Imagine chopping up an element into smaller and smaller pieces. The smallest piece you can get of an element is an *atom*. Atoms are so incredibly tiny that it's hard to imagine how small they are. If you can imagine how many grains of sand there are on a beach, then that's how many atoms there are in a single grain of sand!

The people who tried to make gold discovered many other elements besides gold. They also learned that elements can come together and form

completely new materials. Elements are like the letters of the alphabet, which combine to make words. For example, iron can combine with oxygen in the air to form a red powder. You know this red powder as *rust*. The smallest part of rust is made of iron and oxygen atoms. Whenever two or more atoms are combined, a *molecule* is formed.

Molecules are bigger than atoms, but they are still incredibly small. Rust is made of molecules, and it is not an element. It is called a *compound*.

Elements combine to form compounds in a chemical reaction. For example, hydrogen reacts with oxygen to form water. This reaction is so strong that there is an explosion. Compounds can also react with one another to make different compounds. The science that discovered elements, compounds, and chemical reactions is called *chemistry*.

WHY DOES AN ICE CUBE FLOAT?

Water gets larger when it freezes.

The ice is larger than the water; therefore, ice is less dense than water. The same amount of matter in a larger volume is less dense than in a smaller volume. And anything that is less dense than water will float in it.

It's a good thing for us that ice floats. If all the floating ice at the North and South poles sank into the sea, the oceans would rise and cover all of the land on Earth. There would be no place for us to live.

Check it out:

Fill a paper or Styrofoam cup so that it is half full of water. Hold the cup up to the light so that you can see the water level. Mark the water level on the outside of the cup with a pen. Put the cup in the freezer. Check the level of the water after it has frozen. It is slightly higher than your mark.

Freezing water can do damage. A closed glass jar full of water can crack when the water freezes and expands. Freezing water in the cracks of a stone makes the cracks larger. This is one way stone is slowly turned into sand. Ice can cause concrete to develop cracks. Cracks are put into sidewalks so they won't form cracks where we don't want them. Ice can also make a road buckle into bumps called frost heaves.

Liquid water can flow from one place to another. It has no special shape. It takes the shape of its container. When water becomes ice, it changes from a liquid to a solid. Ice, like all solids, has its own shape. Water changes to ice when the temperature drops to thirty-two degrees Fahrenheit or zero degrees Celsius. When the temperature is around the freezing point, you need to bundle up before going outside.

Other compounds and elements can change from liquids to solids and then melt and change back from solids to liquids. Gold melts at the very hot temperature of almost 2,000 degrees Fahrenheit, or 1,093 degrees Celsius. Candle wax melts at about 125°F or 51°C. That's a little too hot to touch.

The solids of most materials are denser and take up less space than

their liquids. Solid gold would sink in melted gold. Water is special. It is one of the few kinds of matter on Earth that takes up more space when it is a solid than when it is a liquid.

HOW MUCH DOES AIR WEIGH?

Air seems to be nothing because you can't see it or smell it. But it is a kind of matter. It is just not a very dense kind of matter. And like all matter, air does have weight. How can you tell? When it moves as wind, air can destroy houses and uproot trees. If air weighed nothing, it could not move with a force that can do damage.

It's easy to see that air has weight.

Check it out:

Get two balloons that are the same size. Blow them up to equal size and hang one at each end of a yardstick. Balance the yardstick in the middle on your fingers. Have a friend stick a pin in one balloon. Can you explain why the yardstick suddenly tilts?

Air is a kind of matter called a *gas*. Actually, air is a mixture of several gases, including nitrogen and oxygen. Gases are like liquids because they can flow from one place to another. They also take the shape of their container. But gases fill a container completely no matter how big or small it is. Liquids don't always do this.

Air completely covers the Earth the way an egg white surrounds a yolk. The weight of this air pushes on everything and is called *air pressure*. You can use air pressure to do a trick. Air pressure will hold down a wooden yardstick so that you can break it with a karate chop.

Check it out:

Place a wooden yardstick on a smooth table so that the end is sticking out about four inches past the edge. Spread two open sheets of newspaper over the yardstick on the table. Smooth down the newspaper so that it hugs the yardstick and tabletop. There should be no air between the paper and the tabletop. Quickly bring your fist down on the part of the stick that is sticking out. You can break it with a single blow.

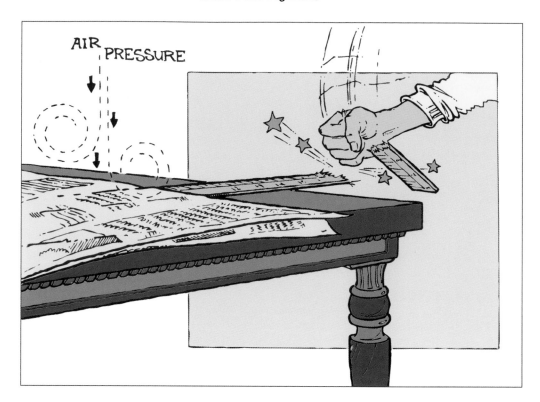

When you move quickly, no air gets under the paper fast enough to make the air pressure underneath equal to the pressure on the surface. Air pressure holds down the paper on the yardstick long enough for you to crack it with your bare hand.

Imagine a long, skinny column of air, five or six miles high over the one-inch box on the previous page. This is the thickness of the layer of air around the Earth. How much do you think that air would weigh? Would you believe about fifteen pounds? So if fifteen pounds presses down on every square inch on the newspaper in our experiment, several tons of air is holding down the paper at the moment you strike the yardstick. If air gets under the paper, it pushes up with the same pressure as it pushes down. Then the paper won't hold the stick in place. So you have to strike quickly without giving the air time to rush underneath.

WHY DON'T YOU FEEL AIR PRESSURE?

You don't feel air pressure because the amount of pressure inside your body that pushes out is exactly the same as the air pressure from the outside pressing in. So the pressure inside your body cancels out the pressure outside your body. But there are times when you *can* feel a change in air pressure. Here's why.

Air is thickest at sea level. It gets thinner as you go up. As air gets less dense, air pressure drops. So air pressure goes down as you go up. When this happens, your body pressure pushes out and your ears feel clogged. You can feel

the change in air pressure when you go up or down in an airplane or elevator. By swallowing, you change the pressure in your ears to make it the same as the outside air pressure.

What would happen if there were suddenly no air pressure? There is no air pressure where there is no air. There is no air on the moon or in space. On Earth, air can be pumped out of a space to make a vacuum. If you were suddenly put in a vacuum, your inside pressure would make you swell up until you burst like a balloon.

HOW IS WARM AIR DIFFERENT FROM COLD AIR?

When you heat air, it expands and takes up more space. So warm air is less dense than colder air and rises above it. Unequal heating makes air move.

You can see warm air rising over a stove. Air rising up a chimney draws the flames upward. Hot air balloons trap heated air and carry passengers up into the sky.

If air expands when it is heated, will it shrink when it is cooled?

What happens when air is heated in a closed container? If the heated air can't expand, it pushes harder and harder on the walls of the container. In other words, as the temperature goes up, so does the pressure. If the pressure becomes too strong for the container, there will be an explosion.

Check it out:

Blow up three identical balloons so they are all the same size. Put one in the freezer, one in the refrigerator, and leave one in the kitchen. After two hours, put all three balloons side by side. Which one is the biggest and which one is the smallest?

WHY ISN'T THE EARTH EGG-SHAPED OR A CUBE?

The shape of the Earth, sun, moon, and stars tells us a lot about matter. These bodies are all shaped like balls. They are called *spheres*. The first thing to remember about each of these bodies is that they contain atoms and molecules that are attracted to each other. If they didn't attract each other, these tiny particles could not have amassed the large collection of matter needed to become what they are now—an Earth or a moon.

The second thing to remember about a sphere is that, at one time, its matter was a fluid, which could flow and become the shape it now has. A fluid takes the shape of a sphere if there are no other forces acting on it.

Oil and water are two kinds of liquids that don't mix. Shake and

Check it out:

Put some vegetable oil in an empty olive or mayonnaise jar. Fill the jar up to an inch below the top. Put drops of food coloring into the oil. Put in big drops and little drops. Watch as they all form spheres and sink slowly to the bottom. Beautiful! At the bottom, the drops flatten out because of gravity. But as they are falling through the oil, all the forces around each drop are equal. It's as if there are no forces around to distort the drops. They will always be spheres.

Screw on the top of the jar. Give one hard shake. Now you have broken up the colored water into hundreds of drops. Can you find one drop hanging in the oil that is not a sphere?

shake your experiment and you will make *millions* of tiny drops of water suspended in the oil. It will look as if the two liquids have mixed. But if you check closely with a magnifying lens, you will see that you've only created very tiny drops of colored water now suspended in the oil.

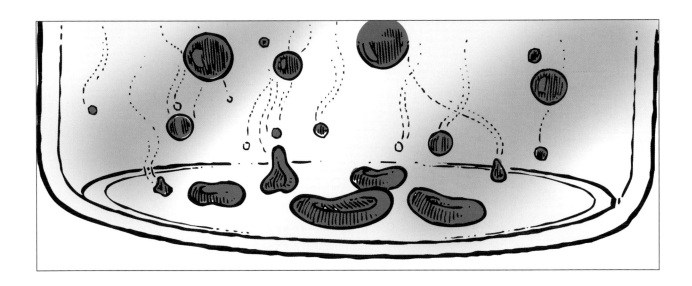

The sphere is nature's most perfect shape. It contains the most volume with the smallest surface. But the Earth is not a perfect sphere. The Earth spins like a top, and this makes the Earth flatter at the poles and wider at the equator.

HOW DOES WOOD BURN?

When wood burns, it seems to disappear. But it really doesn't. It changes into other forms of matter. Burning is a *chemical reaction*. Wood is made up mostly of very large molecules of carbon and hydrogen. When wood burns, the molecules break up. Then the carbon and hydrogen atoms react with oxygen in the air to make carbon dioxide and water. During this reaction, lots of energy is given off as heat and light. The carbon dioxide and water disappear into the air. And the part of the wood that doesn't burn is left behind as ashes.

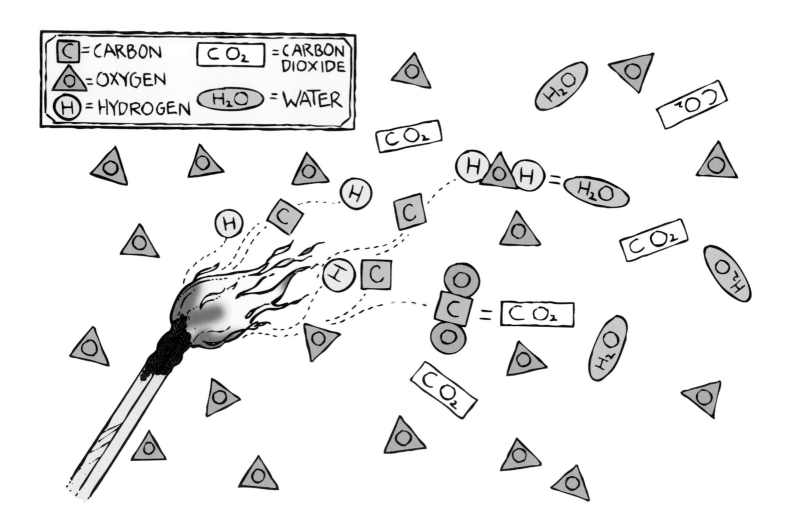

You can make carbon dioxide in another chemical reaction.

Check it out:

Put a pinch of baking soda in a glass of orange juice. The baking soda reacts with a part of the juice. Bubbles form and rise to the surface. The bubbles are carbon dioxide gas. This chemical reaction makes a kind of orange soda.

A BAKING CAKE IS A HOTBED OF REACTIONS.

There are zillions of chemical reactions taking place everywhere. Lots of them are going on in your own body right now. In fact you are a walking factory of chemical reactions. The oxygen you breathe and the food you eat go through chemical reactions to give you energy and help you grow and move and think. Whenever there is a chemical reaction, the matter you end up with is very different from the matter you started with. Can you name some other chemical reactions?

WHY CAN'T YOU UNSCRAMBLE AN EGG?

Eggs are made up of very large, delicate molecules called *proteins.* Egg protein molecules are like tiny balls of yarn. Beating eggs to scramble them unravels the molecules. It would be impossible to wind them back up. When you heat the egg, there is a chemical reaction. The egg white changes from a clear goo into a white solid. This change is permanent. It happens when the egg is boiled or poached or fried, as well as when it's scrambled.

All living things are made of proteins, including you. Proteins are the most important kinds of molecules for life. Proteins help you move and grow and use energy to do all the things you do. When proteins get cooked, they can't do their jobs. That's what happens if you are burned, even sunburned. Proteins are made in your body by chemical reactions. Your body must keep up its supply of proteins and make new ones as you grow.

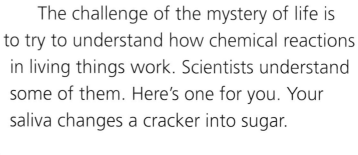

The challenge of the mystery of life is to try to understand how chemical reactions in living things work. Scientists understand some of them. Here's one for you. Your saliva changes a cracker into sugar.

Check it out:

The part of the cracker the saliva works on is not sweet. It is called a starch. Chew a saltine. Hold the chewed cracker in your mouth. Stir it with your tongue. After a while it will start tasting sweet. The saliva has changed the starch into sugar.

Saliva contains a special protein called an *enzyme*, which changes starch to sugar. If you couldn't change starch to sugar, you couldn't get energy from carbohydrates.

If there were no chemical reactions there would be no life on Earth.

WHAT MAKES A LIVING THING A LIVING THING?

6

What do you do that shows you're alive? One thing you do is think. But you don't have to think to be alive. Plants don't think, and earthworms don't have enough brains to do that. So life has to be described in other ways. Scientists have decided that there are certain activities a living thing, or *organism,* does. Here's what they say:

Motion. You can see an animal move from one place to another. But a plant is not capable of moving in the same way. Although all living things move, the kind of motion they share cannot be seen without a microscope. When you look at living material under a microscope, you can see fluid moving from one place to another. This fluid is called *cytoplasm*. Its motion shows that an organism is alive.

Responsiveness. All living things must be able to sense whether conditions are threatening their lives or are favorable. All organisms need a certain amount of warmth, food, and water. Many organisms depend on oxygen for survival, although some use other gases that are poisonous to us. By sensing their surroundings, living things get what they need to survive and also avoid dangers.

Metabolism. A living organism is a very highly organized and complicated structure. It is made of a countless variety of molecules including *proteins*, *fats*, and *carbohydrates*. (A molecule is a group of atoms. An atom is the smallest unit of an element such as carbon, hydrogen, or oxygen.) Proteins are very large molecules that are the building blocks of muscle, bone, blood, and other tissues in your body. In addition, some proteins are enzymes—molecules that control all the chemical reactions in anything alive. Scientists chose the word protein (meaning "of first importance") because they realized that proteins are necessary for life. Fats and carbohydrates are simpler molecules than proteins. They are used for food storage, among other jobs.

In order to maintain such a high level of organization, an organism needs energy. It also needs new materials for growth and repair. The source of energy and building materials for ongoing life is food. *Metabolism* is the sum of all the chemical activity of an organism. The activities of metabolism include getting food, digesting the food, making and repairing cytoplasm, burning food for energy, and getting rid of wastes.

Death occurs when metabolism can no longer be kept going.

Reproduction. If organisms did not reproduce, life could not continue. Every living thing on Earth comes from other living things. So how did the first living thing on Earth appear? Could original life have come from nonliving chemicals?

There have been lots of guesses about how life began, but the best guess is that it began about three and a half billion years ago. Conditions on Earth at that time were very different from what they are now. There was no oxygen in the air. In fact, the atmosphere was made up of methane gas (which is used as fuel today), ammonia gas, and water vapor. The gases in this primitive atmosphere reacted with one another to form complicated molecules that fell into the oceans, making a kind of rich soup. The molecules in the oceans somehow became organized into simple living things. These earliest organisms became the ancestors of all the life that exists on Earth today.

Answer to the question: "How Do We Know Lichens Are Alive?"
Lichens do all the things living things do: They have streaming cytoplasm, they are responsive to the environment, and they metabolize and reproduce. But don't waste your time watching them grow. Most grow a tenth of an inch a year. Lichens grow ten times more slowly in the Arctic than here, so a large patch there may be as much as four thousand years old.

WHAT IS THE SMALLEST LIVING THING?

Since the smallest living thing can't be seen with the naked eye, it couldn't be discovered until the microscope was invented. This was about four hundred years ago, when a Dutch spectacle maker, Zacharias Janssen (YAN-sin) (c.1580–1638), first put two lenses together to act as a magnifier.

In April of 1663, Robert Hooke (1635–1703), an English biologist, placed a very thin slice of cork under a microscope. He invited others to look at the tiny boxlike structures that made up the body of the plant. He called each little structure a *cell* because it reminded him of the tiny rooms in monasteries where monks lived.

Not until almost two hundred years later did scientists discover that cells are important. After looking at different kinds of living things under the microscope, scientists realized that all living things are made of cells. The cell is the smallest unit of life. It performs all the previously listed activities that define life. Cells reproduce: All cells come from other cells. Each cell in a multicelled organism, like a human, metabolizes, responds to its surroundings, and has moving cytoplasm.

Single-celled organisms are the smallest living things. Algae are one-celled plants. Some kinds of algae

form a scum on the surface of ponds. Protozoa are one-celled animals you can find in a drop of pond water and other watery habitats. Bacteria are single cells that live off other organisms, both living and dead. The smallest

one-celled organism is a bacterium that causes pneumonia. The largest single cell is an eight-inch ostrich egg.

Viruses are even smaller than bacteria. But some scientists argue that they are not true organisms because they can only reproduce themselves when they have invaded other cells. In other words, viruses are only "alive" when they are inside other living cells.

Multi-celled plants and animals are made up of many different kinds of cells that do specific jobs. They have skin cells, root cells, blood cells, stem cells, muscle cells, bone cells, nerve cells, and lots more. Scientists have asked many questions about cells, such as, "What do cells look like? How do they do their jobs?"

EXPERIMENT!

1. PULL OFF THIN INSIDE SKIN OF AN ONION.

2. PLACE A PIECE ON A WHITE SURFACE.

3. LOOK THROUGH A MAGNIFIER.

Check it out:

You can see the living cells of an onion with an inexpensive magnifier. Some have a light on them and magnify thirty times actual size. With a pair of tweezers, pull off the thin skin on the inside surface of an onion layer. Place a tiny piece of the skin on a white surface. You can make out the cell walls through your magnifier. The cell walls are lined with a thin *cell membrane*, which can't be seen with your magnifier. But you may be able to see a small, round, membrane-enclosed body in the center of each cell. This is called the *nucleus*.

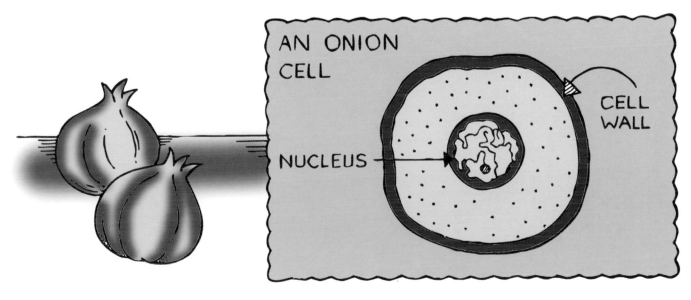

AN ONION CELL

NUCLEUS

CELL WALL

When Robert Hooke first saw the cork cells, he was looking at the *cell walls* of dead plant cells that contained no cytoplasm.

Every plant cell has a cell wall in addition to a cell membrane. Animal cells do not have cell walls. They are enclosed only by a thin cell membrane.

Answer to the question: "What's the largest organism in the world?"

The largest organism in the world is a multi-celled fungus that grows under the forest floor in Oregon. It's called the honey mushroom or shoestring rot. It covers more than 2,000 acres, may weigh more than 600 tons, and is about 2,400 years old. This humongous fungus is the record holder both for the largest living thing and for one of the oldest.

WHY ARE PLANTS GREEN?

Questions that begin with "why" are often too hard for scientists to answer. They prefer questions they can answer by doing experiments. "What are the activities of green plants that keep them alive?" is the kind of question scientists like. The beginning of the answer to this question was discovered in the eighteenth century by Joseph Priestley (1733–1804), an English scientist. Priestley learned that, during the day, green plants take up carbon dioxide from the air and give off oxygen. When we breathe, we do just the opposite: We take up oxygen and give off carbon dioxide. Plants act like us at night, when there is no light.

JOSEPH PRIESTLEY

Another question scientists once asked was, "What is the green stuff in plants and can we get it out?" Back in 1817, two French scientists extracted the pigment that makes plants green. They called it *chlorophyll* from two Greek words meaning "green leaf." They removed the chlorophyll by grinding up spinach with sand and mixing it with alcohol. Then they filtered the ground-up leaves and sand, keeping the liquid.

Check it out:

With the help of an adult, you can also remove chlorophyll. Chop fresh spinach in a food processor or blender. Add rubbing alcohol to extract the chlorophyll. Strain the mixture, keeping the liquid. Try other green plants, such as romaine lettuce or carrot tops. See if the greens are all the same color or if they are slightly different.

Many scientists experimented to find out just how plants make food. They figured out that plants use water from the soil, carbon dioxide from the air, and energy from sunlight to make sugar, a basic food and the simplest carbohydrate:

water + carbon dioxide ⟶ sugar + oxygen

They call this process *photosynthesis*, which means "putting together with light." So, green plants do two very important things: They make food from simple substances, and they replace the oxygen in the air.

But how does chlorophyll fit into photosynthesis? Here are some of the things scientists have learned:

With few exceptions, only green plants make food. Fungi use food made by green plants.

A leaf that is green and white only makes food where the green parts are.

A green plant that's kept in the dark for several days stops making food.

So they concluded that chlorophyll makes photosynthesis possible. Its job is to capture the energy of the light. This energy is then used by plant cells to manufacture food. Since green plants make food, other organisms must either eat green plants or eat living things that eat green plants. Green plants are at the bottom of a chain of food. Without green plants, all other kinds of living things would not exist.

WHY IS BLOOD RED?

Ever notice that hamburger is sometimes bright red and sometimes dark red? You can do an experiment to show how this happens.

Check it out:

Open a package of fresh hamburger meat. The outside should be bright red. Break off a piece. Look at the color of the inside meat. If it has been ground recently, it will also be bright red. But if it has been in the package for a while, it will be dark red. Expose the dark red meat to the air for about a half hour. Does it change color? Something in the meat combines with oxygen in the air to change its color to bright red.

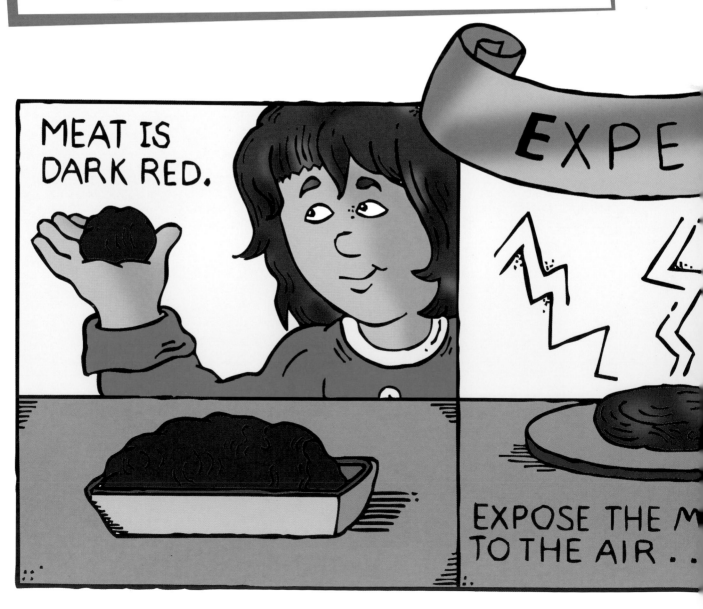

Blood in your body is dark red in your veins and bright red in your arteries. Do you know why this is so? Bright red blood contains oxygen, which you take into your lungs when you breathe. Arteries deliver oxygen-rich blood to all parts of your body. Veins return oxygen-poor blood to the heart, which pumps it to the lungs to pick up another load. Oxygen is actually carried by a red pigment, called *hemoglobin*, which is inside the red blood cells. Each hemoglobin molecule has an atom of iron, which combines with oxygen to make the blood bright red. (Remember that iron metal rusts when it combines with oxygen in the air and becomes a reddish color.)

Fire is a chemical reaction that releases heat and light energy when oxygen combines with a fuel such as wood or oil. Fats and carbohydrates in your cells

act as fuel for oxygen from your blood. But instead of giving off energy all at once, like a fire, your cells release energy for metabolism slowly, without burning you up. This slow release of energy is controlled by enzymes. There are thousands of different kinds of enzymes and each has a particular job to do.

Normally hydrogen peroxide slowly breaks down into oxygen and water. You see the tiny oxygen bubbles rising to the surface. Catalase in the blood of the meat speeds up this reaction, creating a foam. When you put hydrogen peroxide on a cut the same foam forms because of your blood catalase. Cuts get infected if germs that don't like oxygen are allowed to grow. By flooding a wound with oxygen, you make it harder for these germs to survive.

Check it out:

You can see a blood enzyme, called *catalase*, in action. You will need about a tablespoon of bright red, fresh hamburger meat or liver, and some hydrogen peroxide solution. (Hydrogen peroxide is available in the first aid section of any drugstore.) Fill half of a small glass with the hydrogen peroxide. Hold the glass up to the light. Can you see tiny bubbles in the liquid? Put the meat into the glass. Watch what happens to the bubbles.

HOW ARE ALL LIVING THINGS ALIKE?

If you look at fresh, living cells under the microscope, the nucleus is sometimes hard to see. The cells and all their parts are almost transparent. In the 1870s, a German scientist named Walther Flemming (1843–1905) added a chemical dye to the cells under the microscope. He noticed that the nucleus took up more dye than the cell body. So he called the material in the nucleus *chromatin*, from a Greek word meaning "color."

Flemming dyed cells from some rapidly growing animal tissue. Cells grow by repeatedly dividing in two. He discovered that the dye killed the cells at different stages of division. It was like looking at the jumbled still photos of a movie. With careful study, he figured out the order of the pictures so he understood the sequence of cell division.

A CELL DIVIDING

CHROMOSOMES

MY MEMOIRS

Chemical DYE

WALTHER FLEMMING

First, the chromatin suddenly gets organized into a string of oddly shaped beads. These beadlike structures are called *chromosomes*, which mean "colored bodies." Chromosomes have the amazing ability to construct exact copies of themselves using small molecules found in cytoplasm. Each step in the copying process is controlled by enzymes. In this way, they double their number just before a cell divides in two. After cell division, each new cell contains a full set of chromosomes. All cells have chromosomes, but you can only see them when dividing cells have been dyed.

What are chromosomes made of? What do they do inside a cell? These questions kept scientists busy for more than a hundred years after Flemming. This is what they discovered:

All living things have chromosomes in their cell nuclei. Chromosomes are made up of extremely large molecules with a very long name—deoxyribonucleic (dee-OX-ee-rye-bo-new-clay-ic) acid—or DNA, for short. If you could stretch one DNA molecule, it would look like a ladder that has been twisted into a spiral. A *gene* is a section of DNA along a chromosome. Each gene is a master plan that tells the cell how to make a particular protein, including enzymes. Since proteins are the most important molecules, it's fair to say that any organism is the result of all its proteins. So the sum of all the genes equals the total plan for an individual.

How can DNA hold the plans for the tens of thousands of proteins that make up an organism? It turns out that DNA, the information molecule, is actually a code. The rungs of a DNA ladder are made up of two different linked pairs of distinctive groups of atoms known by the initials *A*, *T*, *C*, and *G*. *A* always pairs with *T*, and *C* always pairs with *G*. The order of the pairs is the genetic code that is the plan for a protein. How many different combinations can these two pairs make? It's enough to make genetic

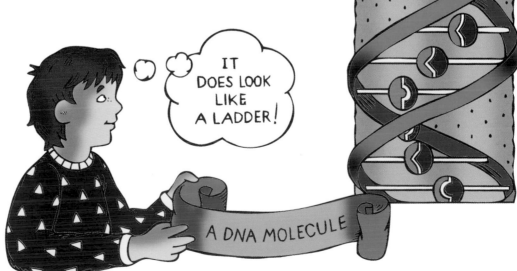

IT DOES LOOK LIKE A LADDER!

A DNA MOLECULE

codes for every characteristic of every living thing on Earth. Amazingly, all organisms, even most viruses, contain DNA.

DNA copies itself when a cell divides. The DNA molecule unzips down its middle, leaving each side of the ladder with a string of half the A-T or C-G pair. Each string then serves as a model to construct its opposite according to the code. For example, a string that is A-T-T-G-C will construct a string that is T-A-A-C-G. In this way, the genes pass on information to the next generation of cells.

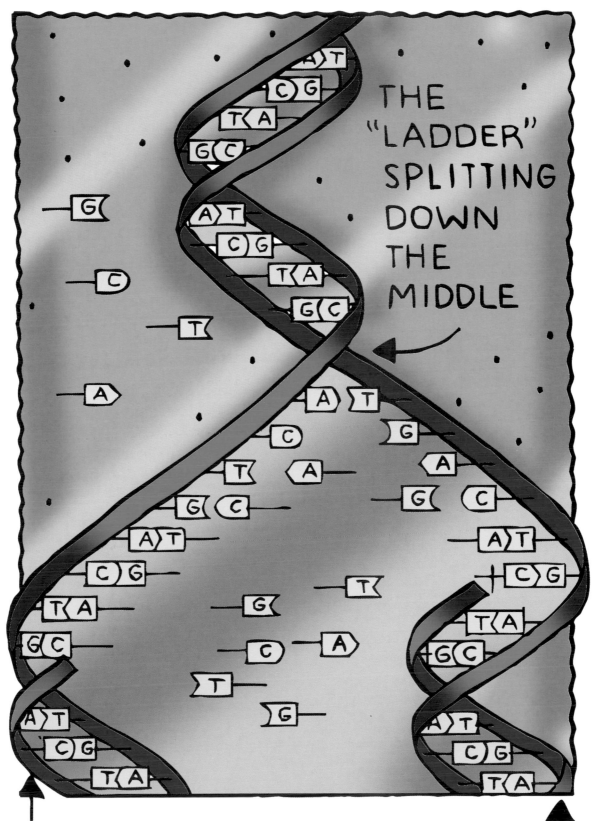

THE "LADDER" SPLITTING DOWN THE MIDDLE

BASES ARE ADDED TO FORM TWO NEW STRANDS.

WHAT MAKES A PEA PLANT A PEA PLANT, A FRUIT FLY A FRUIT FLY, AND A PERSON A PERSON?

A pea plant has fourteen chromosomes, a fruit fly has eight, and a person has forty-six. Chromosomes come in pairs, and every kind of living thing has its own number. So a pea plant has seven pairs, a fruit fly has four, and we have twenty-three. Since chromosomes are made of DNA, it's clear that we have a lot more DNA than either pea plants or fruit flies have. This makes sense. Humans are a lot more complicated than plants or flies. If we could unravel all of the DNA in one of our cells, it would have a length of about six feet. We need many genes, more than twenty thousand, to pass on information. One difference between a pea plant, a fruit fly, and a person is that each has its own set of genes.

Think of it this way: The DNA genetic code is like the letters of the alphabet. The DNA for each species, or kind of living thing, is like a language. Human DNA is a different language than plant DNA or animal DNA. Our DNA tells cells to manufacture the kinds of protein molecules that make us human. It also has the information that decides the color of our eyes, how tall we'll

be, and whether we are male or female. You might think of each person as a separate book. We're all written in the same language, but the details of our stories are different.

Scientists are very familiar with the twenty-three pairs of human chromosomes. They can tell from the chromosomes whether a cell came from a male or a female or if a baby has a certain birth defect. They have also located specific genes on chromosomes—they know their addresses. In 2003 scientists completed a thirteen-year project, called the Human Genome Project, to identify and place all of the 20,000 to 25,000 genes on the twenty-three pairs of human chromosomes. A genome is a layout of all of the DNA in

an organism. Scientists have also figured out the genomes of certain bacteria, a rat, a fish, and the fruit fly, among others. When scientists cracked the code of every gene in a bacterium that causes flu, they found that it has 1,723 genes with almost two million A-T and G-C pairs. Understanding how this relatively simple cell lives can shed light on other cells, including human ones.

WHY CAN'T I LIVE FOREVER?

We all understand the human life cycle: We are born, we grow up, we have children, and we grow old and die. But the simplest living things, which are only one cell, are different. Instead of growing old and dying, they split and become two cells, called *daughter cells*. Then the two daughter cells become four, four become eight, and so on. Each daughter cell has exactly the same DNA as the cell it came from. This kind of cell division is a form of *asexual reproduction* because there is only one parent. One-celled organisms can die if they are eaten or suddenly have no water or food. But in their lifecycle, they don't die—they reproduce. Many cells in our bodies reproduce like these single-celled organisms. The DNA in each kind of cell—muscle cell, skin cell, nerve cell—never changes in the daughter cells. Since you were originally a single cell, and all your cells came from that cell, all your cells have exactly the same DNA.

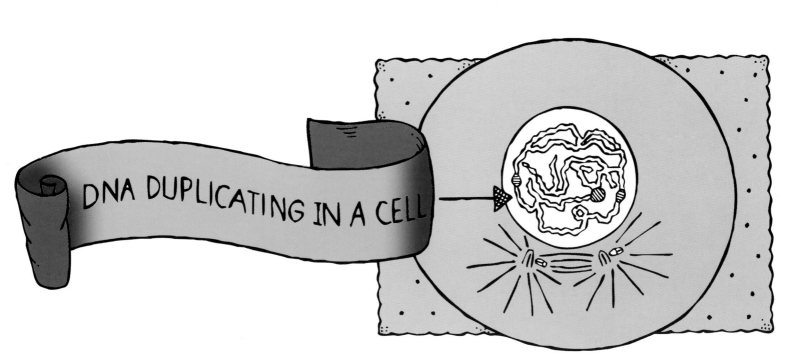

DNA DUPLICATING IN A CELL

More complicated living things, like people, reproduce by *sexual reproduction*. You began when a sperm cell from your father united with an egg cell from your mother. Sperm and egg cells are different from other human cells in a very important way: They each have only twenty-three chromosomes—half a complete set and half the DNA needed to make a person. When a sperm enters an egg, the complete number is restored. So you got half your chromosomes from your father and half from your mother.

The twenty-three pairs of chromosomes are like cards in a deck. When eggs and sperm are formed in your parents' bodies, each pair is split and recombines as if the deck were shuffled. Your brothers and sisters get a different mixture, or "hand," than you do.

You share *some* but not *all* of the chromosomes present in other members of your family. The only people who share exactly the same DNA are identical twins. They are two individuals who developed from a single fertilized egg that became two separate cells. Each cell then became a person.

Shuffling DNA creates many kinds of people. This shuffling ensures that the strongest will survive to reproduce. The human race can keep getting stronger. Individuals die. But DNA can get passed along for generations to come.

Check it out:

You might want to make a family tree to show where some trait, like a dimple or eye color, got passed on from one person to another. The entire family might have fun choosing which traits to follow.

HOW LONG CAN WE LIVE?

Officially, the oldest person to have ever lived was Jeanne Calment (1875–1997) of France, who died at the age of 122 years, 164 days. How was she doing at the end of her life? She didn't hear very well, she couldn't walk, and she couldn't see. But she thought that was normal for her age. When she was only 100, she was still riding her bicycle around town. Most people can expect to live about seventy-five to eight-five years. If we could keep our bodies as fresh and new as they are at two years old, we could easily last a hundred years.

Scientists have wondered about how long we can live. They have grown human cells in the laboratory. These cells die after about seventy cell divisions. What causes this? Is there a gene that acts like a clock? We don't know. Some cells in our body live longer than others. We don't know why. Are there genes that protect the cells of the body? If we discovered them, could we someday eliminate disease as a cause of death? No one knows. We know that living a

long time is inherited and that our body parts wear out as we age, just like an old car. Jeanne Calment's mother lived to eight-six and her father lived to ninety-three. Obviously her body parts have the genes to make them last. But we don't know how.

What is the ideal way to die at the end of a long life? We aren't really sure, but we think that a person can stay healthy and active until the day he or she dies. Death is a natural part of the life process.

S.S. DNA

A LONG LIFE TO ALL!

SCIENTIFIC TERMS

Air pressure The weight of the atmosphere on a surface. At sea level the air pressure is about 15 pounds per square inch.

Asexual reproduction A method of reproduction that involves only one parent. Simple one-celled plants and animals divide in half to produce two daughter cells. Cells in multi-celled organisms reproduce this way when tissues grow.

Atom The smallest particle of an element.

Carbohydrates Sugar and starch molecules manufactured by plants in the process of photosynthesis. They serve as the bottom of the food chain and are the food source for all animals and plants.

Catalase A blood enzyme that helps break down hydrogen peroxide into water and oxygen.

Cell The basic unit of life. All living things, from one-celled bacteria to multi-celled humans, are made of cells.

Cell membrane The thin skin that encloses the cell.

Cell wall The semi-rigid nonliving structure that is outside the cell membrane of plant cells.

Center of gravity The point of a body where all of its mass seems to be concentrated. When an object falls, it is most stable and least likely to tip over when its center of gravity is closest to the center of the Earth.

Centrifugal force A force that is only present when an object is rotating around a central point, such as the moon rotating around the Earth or a ball whirling on a handheld string. It holds the object away from the center.

Chemical reaction The change in a material when compounds are formed or broken up. All chemical reactions either take up energy or give it off.

Chemistry The science that studies elements, compounds, and chemical reactions.

Chlorophyll A green plant pigment that absorbs energy from the sun. It enables plants to make sugar from carbon dioxide and water.

Chromatin The material in the nucleus of cells that picks up a chemical dye and becomes colored under the microscope. Chromatin is organized into chromosomes during cell division.

Chromosomes The tiny bodies in the cell nucleus that become visible during cell division. Chromosomes are made up of DNA. In sperm and egg cells, chromosomes carry the hereditary information that is passed on to offspring.

Compound The combination of two or more elements to make a completely different material. Water is a compound of hydrogen and oxygen.

Constellations Groups of stars that make patterns in the sky.

Cytoplasm The living material of cells.

Daughter cells The two cells produced by asexual reproduction (cell division).

Density The amount of matter packed into a specific volume.

DNA Short for deoxyribonucleic acid, long threadlike molecules that contain the genetic codes needed for life. All organisms have DNA.

Element Matter that can not be broken down into a simpler material. There are ninety-two naturally occurring elements on Earth.

Energy The ability to do **work** (a scientific term). It includes light, sound, electricity, heat, chemical, and kinetic (motion).

Enzymes Proteins that control all the chemical reactions of living things.

Fats Molecules made by living things from carbohydrates; energy-rich food stored within the organism.

First Law of Motion Moving objects will move forever in a straight line and resting objects will rest forever, unless some outside force acts on them.

Friction A force that occurs between two surfaces where there is motion. It works against that motion.

Gas A kind of matter that has no definite shape and no definite volume. It takes both the volume and shape of its container.

Gene A section of DNA along a chromosome. Each gene is a master plan for making one protein. Each gene controls some specific trait that is passed on to future generations.

Gravity The force of attraction between two bodies of matter, such as the Earth and the moon, or the Earth and you.

Heat conductors Materials that become hot very quickly, like metals.

Heat insulators Materials that do not heat up easily but absorb heat, like Styrofoam.

Hemoglobin The red pigment in blood. It is responsible for carrying oxygen to all the cells of the body.

Inertia The resistance an object has to being moved. Heavier objects have more inertia than lighter ones.

Infrared Invisible light on the red end of the visible spectrum. It is absorbed by objects in the sun and makes them feel warm.

Liquid A kind of matter that takes the shape of its container but not its volume.

Metabolism All of the chemical reactions of an organism that keep it alive. An organism is constantly taking in molecules from the environment and giving off waste. The activities of metabolism include getting food, digesting the food, making and repairing cytoplasm, burning food for energy, and getting rid of wastes.

Microwaves Invisible light next to infrared radiation that can make water boil in a microwave oven.

Molecule A combination of two or more atoms.

Nuclear fusion The fusing of the nuclei of two hydrogen atoms to produce one helium atom. The helium nucleus weighs slightly less than the two hydrogen nuclei and this difference is given off as an enormous amount of energy. It is the source of the sun's energy.

Nucleus (nuclei, plural) The membrane-enclosed body in the center of a cell. It contains the DNA that directs all the activities of the cell. It can also be an atomic nucleus, or the center of an atom.

Organism Any independent living thing, plant, or animal.

Parallax The apparent shift of position of the foreground compared to the background due to a shift in the position of the observer. **Ocular** parallax is the different view of background and foreground from each eye**. Stellar** parallax is the shift in the star patterns due to the different positions of the earth in its orbit during the year. If you have a hard time visualizing how this works, Google "stellar parallax" (with help from an adult). There are a number of clear animations on the Web to illustrate the idea.

Pendulum A freely swinging object.

Photosynthesis The process by which green plants manufacture sugar, using water, carbon dioxide, and energy from the sun.

Proteins Large, complicated molecules essential for life. The living material of organisms is mostly protein.

Radioactivity The breakdown of heavy atoms, such as uranium, to give off a variety of penetrating and sometimes dangerous rays.

Sexual reproduction Reproduction that involves two parents. A new individual begins when a sperm cell and an egg cell unite.

Sphere Nature's most perfect shape. It contains the most volume with the smallest surface.

Species A kind of plant or animal. Human beings are species.

Spectrum The colors of the rainbow when white light is broken up into its parts: red, orange, yellow, green, blue, and violet.

Ultraviolet light Invisible light on the violet end of the spectrum. It can burn skin if you are overexposed to sunlight.

Weight The force of gravity on an object.

Work Force used to move an object.

X-rays Invisible light next to ultraviolet that can pass through solid materials and reveal what is inside.

INDEX

FOR FURTHER READING

Balkwill, Frances R., and Mic Rolph. *Enjoy Your Cells*. Cold Spring Harbor: Cold Spring Harbor Laboratory Press, 2001.

Bang, Molly and Penny Chisholm. *Living Sunlight: How Plants Bring the Earth to Life*. The Blue Sky Press, 2009.

Brown, Don. *Odd Boy Out, Young Albert Einstein*. Boston: Houghton Mifflin, 2004.

Cobb, Vicki, and Josh Cobb. *Light Action! Amazing Experiments with Optics*. Bellingham: SPIE Press, 2005.

Cobb, Vicki. *Fireworks* (Where's the Science Here? Series). Minneapolis: Lerner Books, 2006.

Cobb, Vicki. *Your Body Battles a Skinned Knee*. Minneapolis: Millbrook Press, 2009.

Krull, Kathleen. *Isaac Newton*. New York: Viking, 2006.

Oxlade, Chris. *Elements & Compounds*. Chicago: Heinemann Library, 2002.

Panchyk, Richard. *Galileo for Kids: His Life and Ideas, 25 Activities* (For Kids series). Chicago: Chicago Review Press, 2005.

Romanek, Trudee. *Mysterious You: Squirt! The Most Interesting Book You'll Ever Read About Blood*. Toronto: Kids Can Press Ltd, 2006.

Venezia, Mike. *Albert Einstein, Universal Genius*. New York: Children's Press, 2009.

On the Web:
Great videos on YouTube. Search by name if you don't want to copy the link.

Physics for Kids Rutgers U: Rutgers professor Mark Croft has divided up his Christmas lecture for kids into five minute segments. These illustrate concepts well and are a lot of fun to watch.

Newton's Laws:
http://www.youtube.com/watch?v=qKM-08Z6WLo

Energy of Motion:
http://www.youtube.com/watch?v=LWuXPEKFfEU

Sound Waves on Fire:
http://www.youtube.com/watch?v=x7Ygl1eUbys

Cell Biology:This is a 17 minute video with great looks at cells. Well worth the time to watch.
http://www.youtube.com/watch?v=zufaN_aetZI

Photosynthesis song! There are a number of songs about this fundamental process of green plants but this one is the clearest:
http://www.youtube.com/watch?v=tSHmwlZ9FNw

Photosynthesis lets get into this rap lyrics in description: This is a clever rap, and well illustrated, that gives a lot more information than it can explain. But it may be a way to remember the details of the process if you're studying for a test.
http://www.youtube.com/watch?v=Wi60tQa8jfE&feature=related